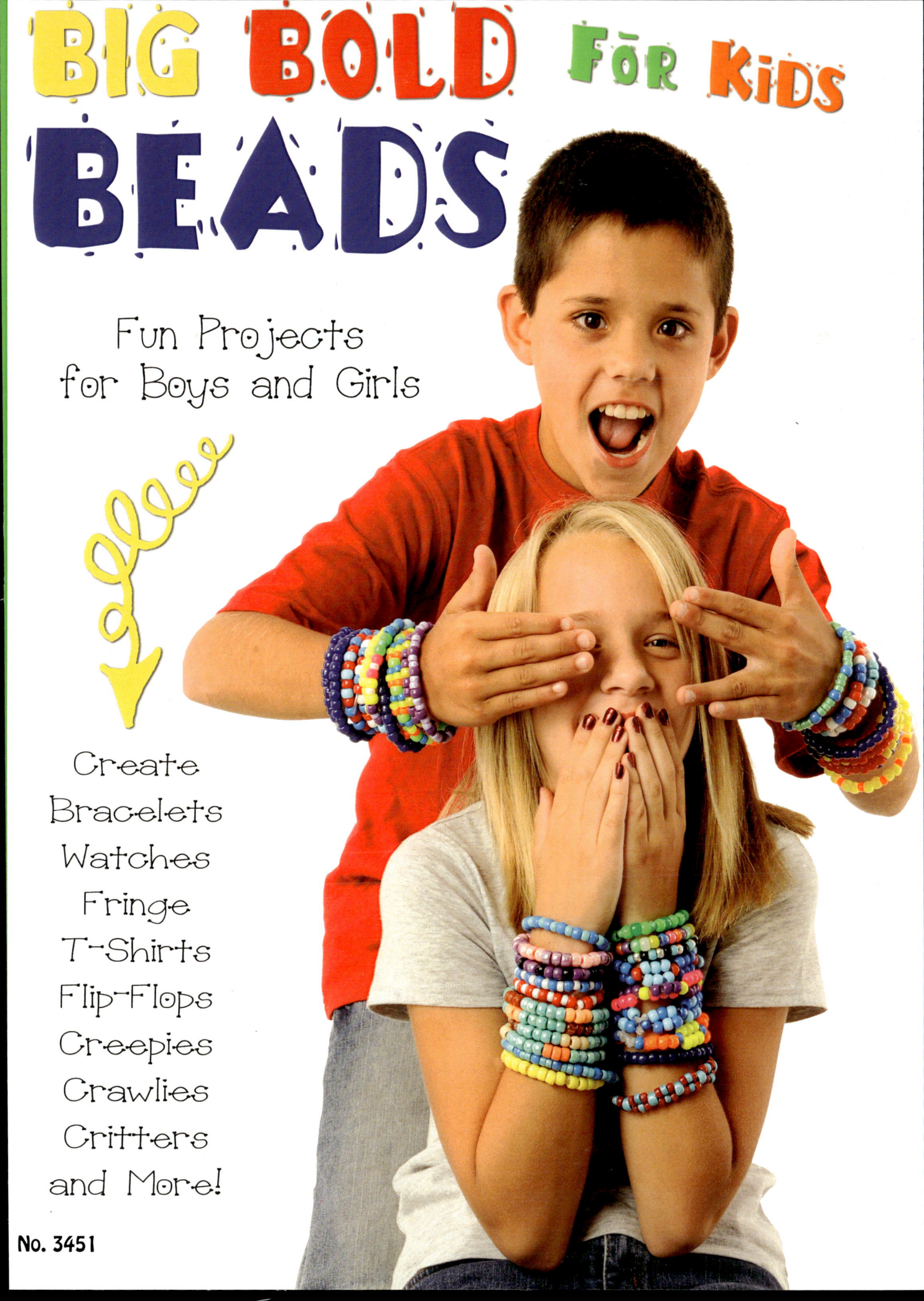

BIG BOLD BEADS

FOR KIDS

Fun Projects for Boys and Girls

Create
Bracelets
Watches
Fringe
T-Shirts
Flip-Flops
Creepies
Crawlies
Critters
and More!

No. 3451

Quick & Easy
Bracelet designs

Big Bold Beads

Everyone I talk to, from the kids next door to my nephew's fourth grade teacher, just love to create projects with Pony Beads!

Bracelets and colorful creatures made from beads and cord are easy enough for children and teens to make. Use them to wear, on a back pack, as a key-chain or just give them to your friends as a special gift.

So gather your supplies and get started making your own projects with big bold beads today!

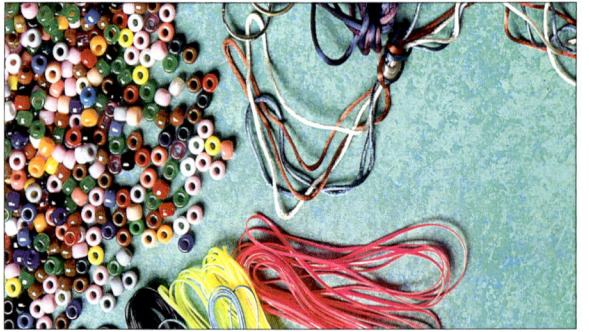

What You'll Need

Some colorful pony beads
Cord (plastic lanyard lace, rattail, elastic or yarn)
Glue (jewelry glue is best)

**WARNING!
CHOKING HAZARD**
Small Parts. Not for children under 3 years.

To learn more about the other great books from Fox Chapel Publishing, or to find a retailer near you, call toll-free 800-457-9112 or visit us at *www.FoxChapelPublishing.com*. We are always looking for talented authors. To submit an idea, please send a brief inquiry to acquisitions@foxchapelpublishing.com.

Printed in the USA

© 2011 DESIGN ORIGINALS by Fox Chapel Publishing, 903 Square Street, Mount Joy, PA 17552.   *www.foxchapelpublishing.com*

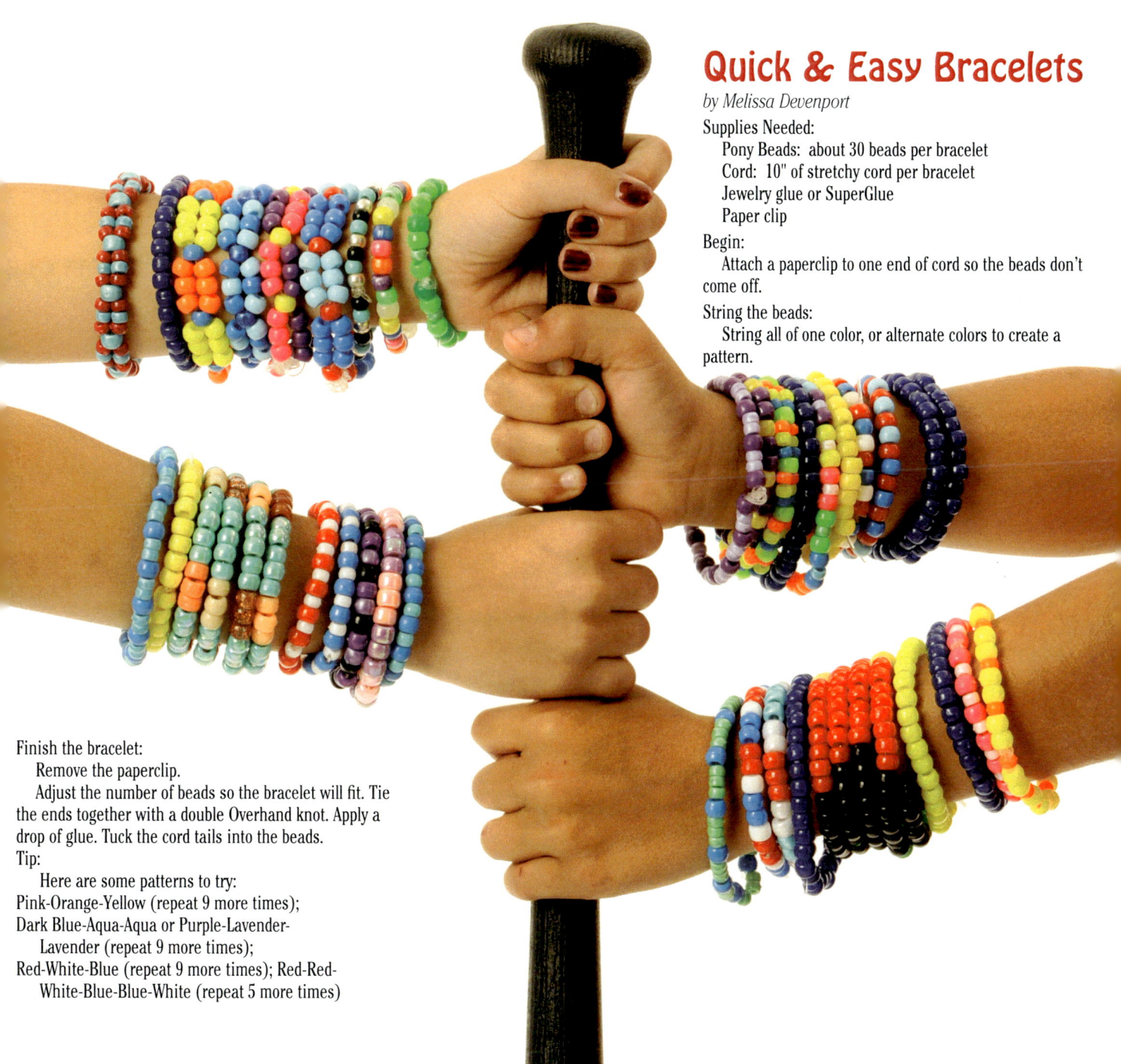

Quick & Easy Bracelets
by Melissa Devenport

Supplies Needed:
Pony Beads: about 30 beads per bracelet
Cord: 10" of stretchy cord per bracelet
Jewelry glue or SuperGlue
Paper clip

Begin:
Attach a paperclip to one end of cord so the beads don't come off.

String the beads:
String all of one color, or alternate colors to create a pattern.

Finish the bracelet:
Remove the paperclip.
Adjust the number of beads so the bracelet will fit. Tie the ends together with a double Overhand knot. Apply a drop of glue. Tuck the cord tails into the beads.

Tip:
Here are some patterns to try:
Pink-Orange-Yellow (repeat 9 more times);
Dark Blue-Aqua-Aqua or Purple-Lavender-
Lavender (repeat 9 more times);
Red-White-Blue (repeat 9 more times); Red-Red-
White-Blue-Blue-White (repeat 5 more times)

Beaded Flip-Flops
by Donna MJ Kinsey

Pony Beads:
36 Yellow, 18 Blue, 18 Aqua, 18 Green
Ribbon: 5 yards of Green sheer ribbon
Begin: Cut 18 ribbons 10" long.
Tie ribbon to flip flop with an Overhand knot, making the ribbon ends even.
Beads: On each end of the ribbon, string a Yellow, Blue, Aqua, Green and Yellow bead.
Finish: Tie two Overhand knots, one over the other to make a knot thick enough so the beads don't come off. Trim ribbon ends as needed.

Basic Steps for Animals

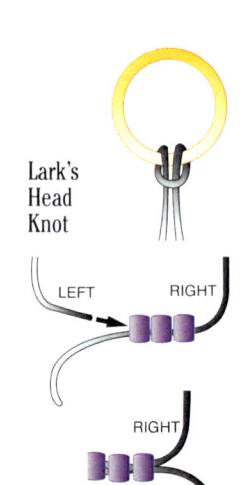

Lark's
Head
Knot

Begin

Cut cord, find the center and mount cord on a key ring or lanyard hook with a Lark's head knot. Or fold cord in half and tie an Overhand knot leaving a loop for hanging.

Row 1 —

String beads for the first row onto the right cord then slide to the center. Weave the left cord, from left to right, through the beads.

Row 2 —

String the second row of beads on the right cord. Weave the left cord, from left to right, through the beads. Continue stringing on the right cord and weaving the left cord through the beads to complete.

Arms, Legs & Wings

String all beads for each appendage on one cord. Bring beads for the outer row out a little way on the cord then bring beads for the next-to-last row out. Weave the cord back through the beads for the next-to-last row and pull to tighten. Bring beads for the next row out and weave the cord through them. Continue until the leg, arm or wing construction is completed.

Beginning at the body, pull cord through, one row at a time, to tighten cord and bring the leg, arm or wing up to the body.

Additional Arms, Legs, Wings

Construct ears, arms, legs, tails and wings following the individual project instructions.

Optional: Use wire in place of cord to make poseable animals and dolls.

Finish

After beading is complete, tie the cord ends in 1-2 Overhand knots to secure the beads. If beads are added to the ending cord tie another knot to secure all added beads.

Overhand Knot

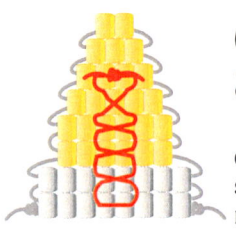

Optional: Support Thread

Occasionally a beaded piece will be loose especially when the beads are strung on soft ribbon or yarn, or when the cords are not pulled taut. Simply weave an extra cord up through the center beads with small cord or with strong thread.

Tip: Wrap the ends of your cord with tape to make a 'point' or dip the ends in white glue and let dry to prevent fraying.

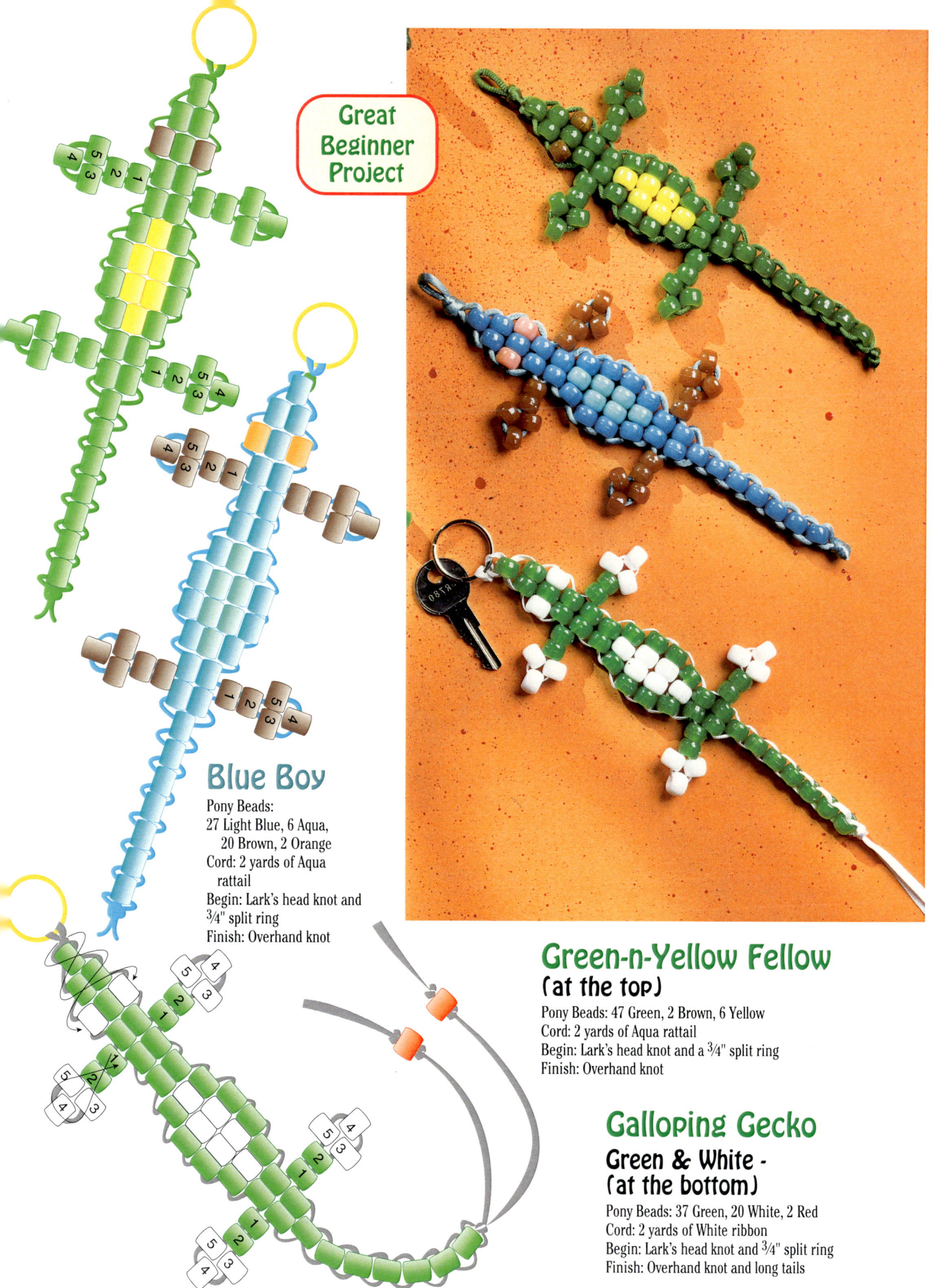

Great Beginner Project

Blue Boy

Pony Beads:
27 Light Blue, 6 Aqua,
20 Brown, 2 Orange
Cord: 2 yards of Aqua
rattail
Begin: Lark's head knot and
¾" split ring
Finish: Overhand knot

Green-n-Yellow Fellow
(at the top)

Pony Beads: 47 Green, 2 Brown, 6 Yellow
Cord: 2 yards of Aqua rattail
Begin: Lark's head knot and a ¾" split ring
Finish: Overhand knot

Galloping Gecko
Green & White - (at the bottom)

Pony Beads: 37 Green, 20 White, 2 Red
Cord: 2 yards of White ribbon
Begin: Lark's head knot and ¾" split ring
Finish: Overhand knot and long tails

Beaded Fringe for Wearables

by Melissa Devenport

Wearables:
    T-shirt, T-shirt scarf
    or Bandana
Scissors
Pony Beads:
    For T-shirt:
        304 Red
        304 White
    For Scarf:
        64 Blue
        48 Pink
        48 Green
        48 Yellow
        48 Purple
        48 Orange
    For Bandana:
        56 Black
        28 White

Begin:
    Cut edge into ½" wide fringe strips.
Beads:
    Thread beads onto each strip of fringe.
Finish:
    Overhand knot
Tip:
    On the T-shirt, we used 6 beads on each bottom fringe and 4 beads on each sleeve fringe.
    For the scarf, we used 8 beads on each fringe.
    To make the bandana, fold on the diagonal to form a triangle. On the hemmed edge (not the fold), start cutting fringe halfway down each side. Cut through both layers. Cut fringe about 2" deep. String 3 beads onto both layers. Separate the layers and tie an Overhand knot.

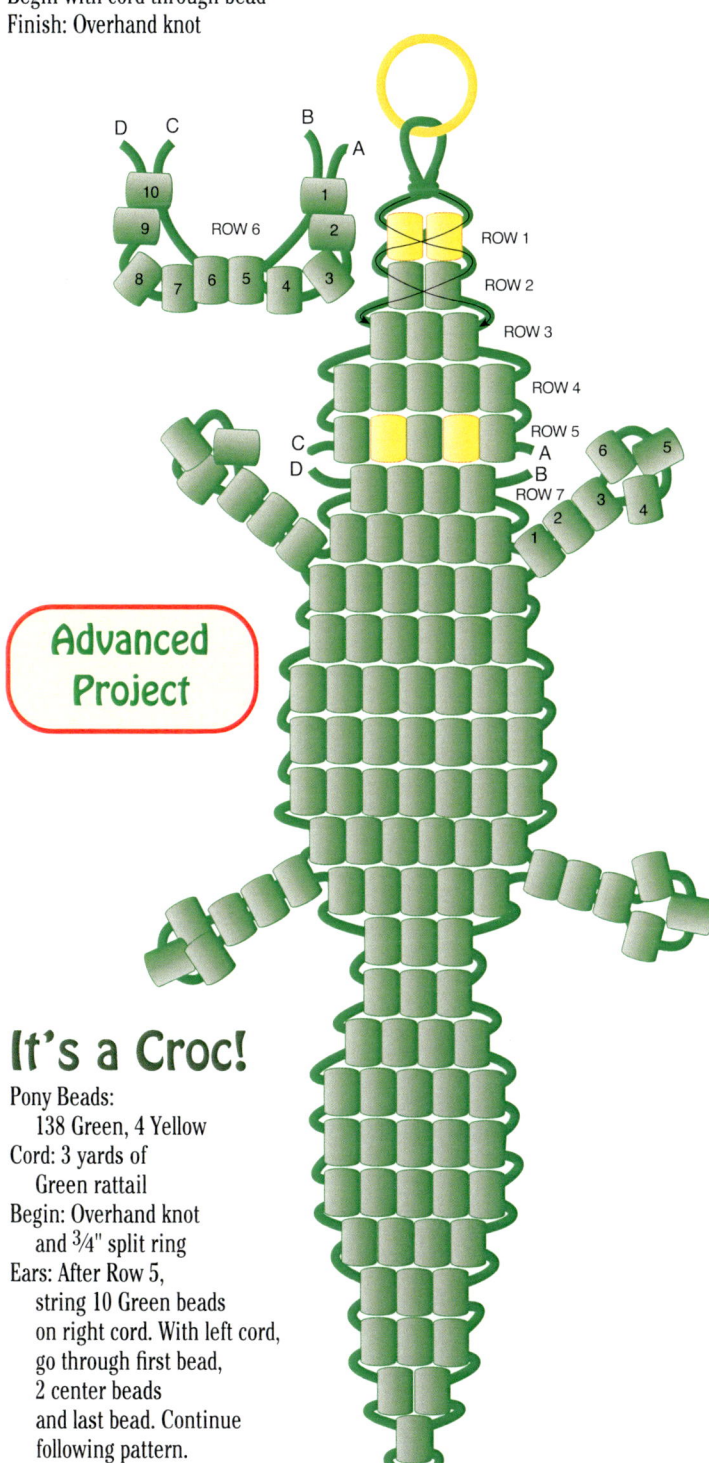

Glow, Little Worm

Pony Beads: 12 Yellow,
   2 Black, 12 Orange, 12 Green,
   12 Blue, 15 Purple
Cord: 2 yards of Green rattail
Begin with cord through bead
Finish: Overhand knot

Great Beginner Project

Advanced Project

It's a Croc!

Pony Beads:
   138 Green, 4 Yellow
Cord: 3 yards of
   Green rattail
Begin: Overhand knot
   and ¾" split ring
Ears: After Row 5,
   string 10 Green beads
   on right cord. With left cord,
   go through first bead,
   2 center beads
   and last bead. Continue
   following pattern.
Finish: Overhand knot

U. Toucan... Can-Can

by Dawn Maier

Pony Beads: 50 Black, 7 Yellow, 13 Neon Orange, 4 Neon Yellow, 5 Neon Green, 24 White

Lace: 2 yards of Black plastic noodle

Begin: Overhand knot and lanyard hook

Beak: Add Neon Orange and Neon Green beads to beak. Add Neon Yellow beads and go back through Neon Green, Neon Orange and Neon Green before adding next row.

Finish: Overhand knots

Drag N. Fly... Flitters Colorfully By

by Virginia Reynolds

Pony Beads:
42 Silver Glitter, 9 Neon Pink, 4 Neon Blue

Lace: 2 yards of Clear plastic lanyard

Begin: Overhand knot and loop

Finish: Tie an Overhand knot at the end of the body. Tie an Overhand knots on both strands of the tails, add beads and tie another Overhand knot.

Frog Legs Freddy...

Pony Beads: 29 Green (body), 30 Neon Green (legs), 12 Orange, 2 Black, 9 Red

Lace: 2 yards of Green plastic lanyard

Begin: Overhand knot and loop

Finish: Overhand knots

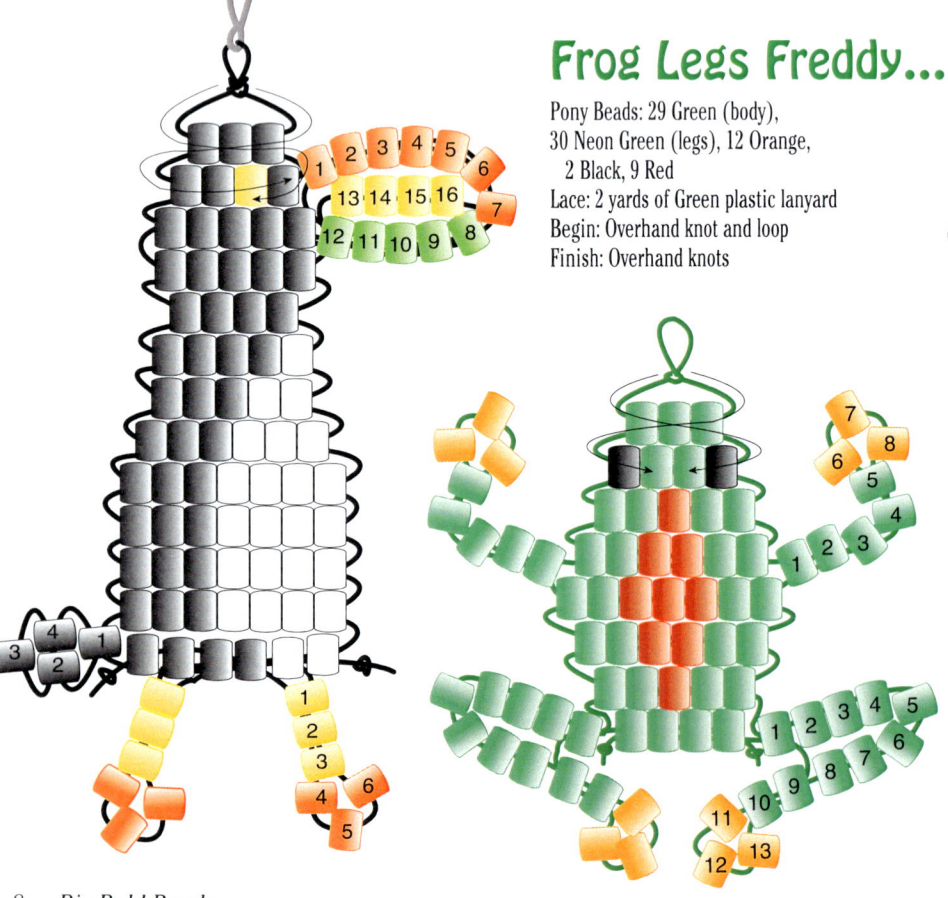

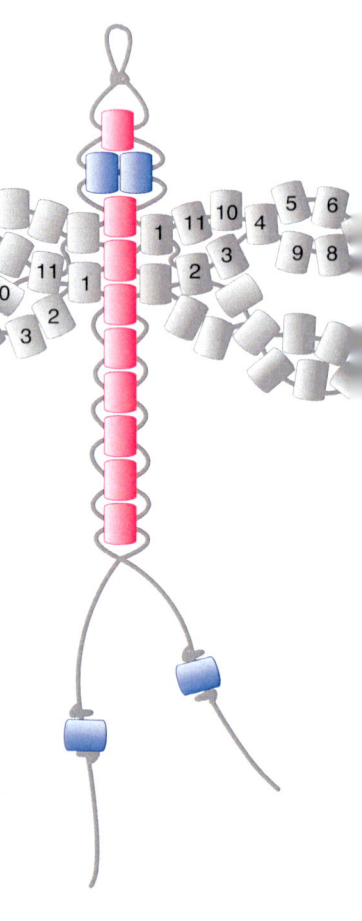

Photo Bracelets & Watches

by Melissa Devenport

For Watch:
  40 Brown and Copper pony beads (mixed)
  Watch face
For Photo Bracelet:
  48 Blue pony beads or 48 Black pony beads
  2 Bracelet Photo frames or 2 small drilled dominoes
Cord: two 15" pieces
  Stretchy cord for each watch or bracelet
Jewelry glue or SuperGlue

Make the Watch:

Pass a cord through one side of the watch and center. On each side, string 10 Brown and 8 Copper beads, alternating them as desired. Tie a double Overhand knot and secure with glue. Tuck the cord tails inside the beads. Repeat for the other side of the watch.

Make the Photo and Domino Bracelets:

Attach a paperclip to the end of 1 cord. String a Silver heart bead and 6 Blue beads. Pass the cord through the top hole of a frame. String 6 Blue beads. Pass cord through the top hole of the second frame. String 6 beads and a Silver heart. Remove the paperclip. Tie a double Overhand knot. Apply a drop of glue to the knot. Thread cord tails through the beads. Repeat for the second cord, passing it through the bottom of the frames.

Finish: Glue photos into the frames with White glue.

Watch design

Domino and photo design

2 Strand Bracelets

Pony Beads:
  8 beads of Color A
  24 beads of Color B
  18 beads of Color C
Cord: two 15" pieces of stretchy
  cord per bracelet
Jewelry glue or SuperGlue
Begin: Tie 2 cords together with an Overhand knot
  leaving 3" tails.
Stringing: Pass both cords through a bead (Color A).
  Separate the cords.
  String 3 beads of Color B onto each cord.
  Pass both cords through a bead (Color A).
  Cross the cords and pull gently to tighten beads.
  Separate the cords.
  String 3 beads of Color C on each cord.
  Pass both cords through a bead (Color A).
  Cross the cords and pull gently.
  Separate cords as before, string 3 beads of Color B.
  Continue alternating colors. End with a Color A bead.
Finish: Adjust the number of beads so the bracelet will fit. Tie the ends together with a double Overhand knot. Apply a drop of glue. Tuck the cord tails into the beads.

2 Strand design

Coiled Wire Bracelets

by Melissa Devenport

Memory Wire with 4 coils for each bracelet
Pony Beads:
  For Aqua Bracelet: 85 Aqua, 9 Copper, 9 Brown, 9 Tan, 9 Peach, 9 Pink
  For Primary Colors Bracelet: 40 Black, 32 Red, 32 Yellow, 32 Green
  Jewelry Pliers
  Jewelry glue or SuperGlue
Start: Turn a loop in one end of the wire so the beads don't fall off.

Aqua Bracelet:

String these beads: 5 Aqua-3 Copper-5 Aqua- 3 Tan-5 Aqua- 3 Pink-5 Aqua- 3 Brown- 5 Aqua- 3 Peach. Repeat until you run out of beads.
Turn a loop in the end of the wire.

Primary Colors Bracelet:

String these beads: 8 Black- 8 Green- 8 Yellow- 8 Red. Repeat until you run out of beads. Turn a loop in the end of the wire.

Big Bold Beads

Start with a simple pattern... the snake, fish, gecko or ladybug, and practice until you get the hang of beading.

Always bead on a flat surface. It's easier to keep count of the beads and they don't get tangled.

Rattle Snake

PONY BEADS:
2 Red	31 Tan
15 Rust	8 Grey

CORD:
2 yards of Tan yarn

Coral Snake

PONY BEADS:
22 Black
17 Red
15 Yellow
CORD:
2 yards of Black yarn

Croc O. Dile

PONY BEADS:
55 Green
13 Green Pearl
2 Orange Crystal
CORD:
2 yards of Green yarn

Daff Giraffe

PONY BEADS:
3 Black
36 Ivory
46 Tortoise
CORD:
2 yards of Ivory yarn

Happy Face

PONY BEADS:
10 Black
34 Yellow
CORD:
2 yards of Yellow yarn

Great Beginner Projects

Quiet Mouse

PONY BEADS:
48 White
11 Pink
2 Red
CORD:
2 yards of White yarn

Brownie Fox

PONY BEADS:
44 Rust
5 White
5 Black
CORD:
2 yards of White yarn

Pinky Pig

PONY BEADS:
43 Pink Pearl
4 Ivory
CORD:
2 yards of Pink yarn

Dead Duck

PONY BEADS:
49 White
15 Yellow
CORD:
2 yards of White yarn

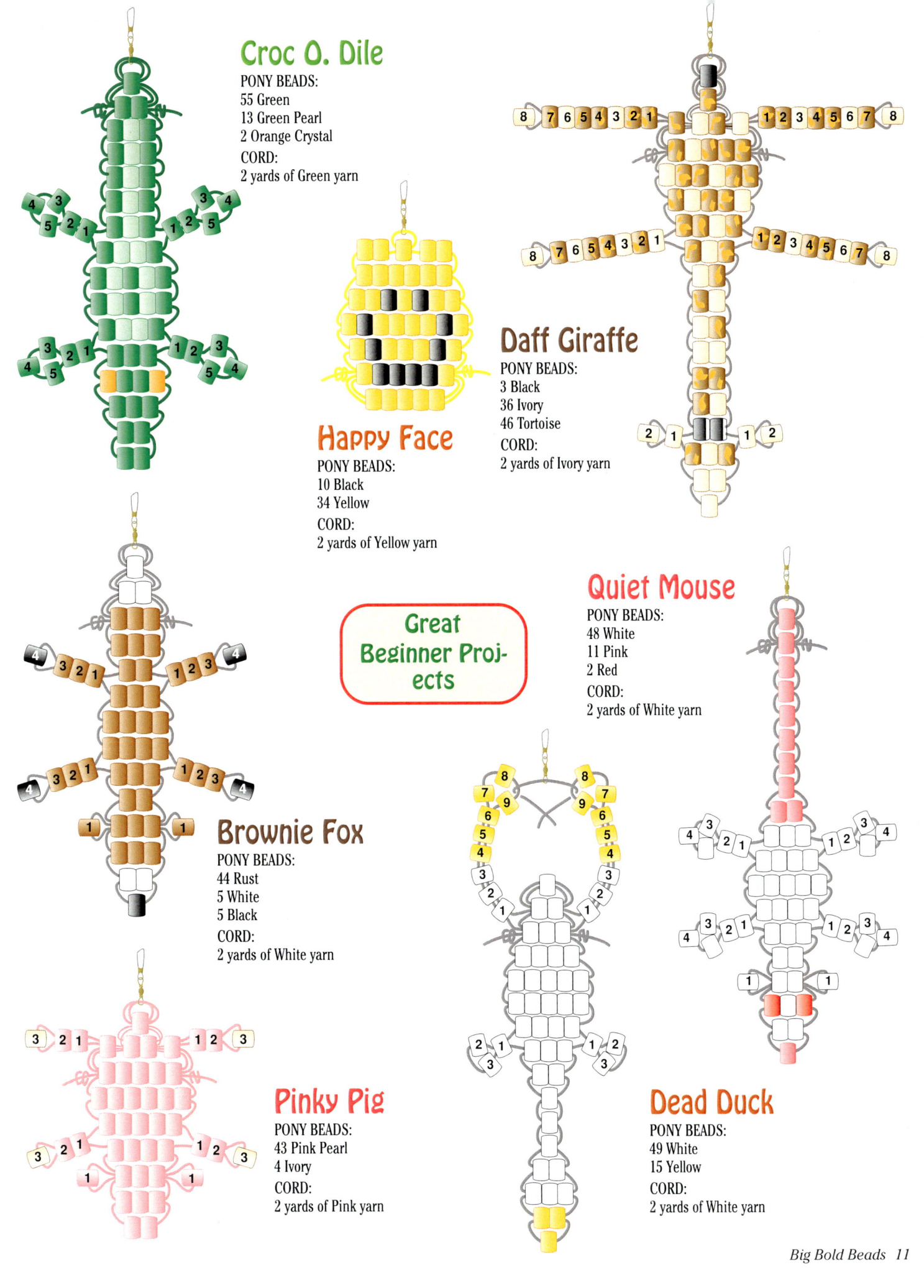

Bookworm

by Bev George

BEADS:
71 Clear Baby Pony Beads
2 Black Baby Pony Beads
1MM Rainbow Elastic:
3 yards of Jade
3 yards of Terracotta
3 yards of Soft Seafoam

WORM: Fold 3 pieces of elastic in half. Make top braid and weave worm with 2 strands of Green on each side. Lace Terracotta down center beads of back. Make bottom braid adding beads.

2¾" BRAID

Dragonfly

FLY: Cut Deep Peacock elastic in half. Fold 3 pieces of elastic in half. Make top braid, tie knot. Weave bug with 2 strands of Dark Peacock elastic on each side. Lace Jade elastic down center beads of back. Tie elastic tails together with an overhand knot. Make bottom braid adding beads.

BEADS:
2 Black Pony
1 Turquoise 6mm Round
30 Turquoise Crystal Pony
57 Beige Crystal Baby Pony
1 MM Rainbow Elastic:
6 yards of Deep Peacock
3 yards of Bright Jade

2" BRAID

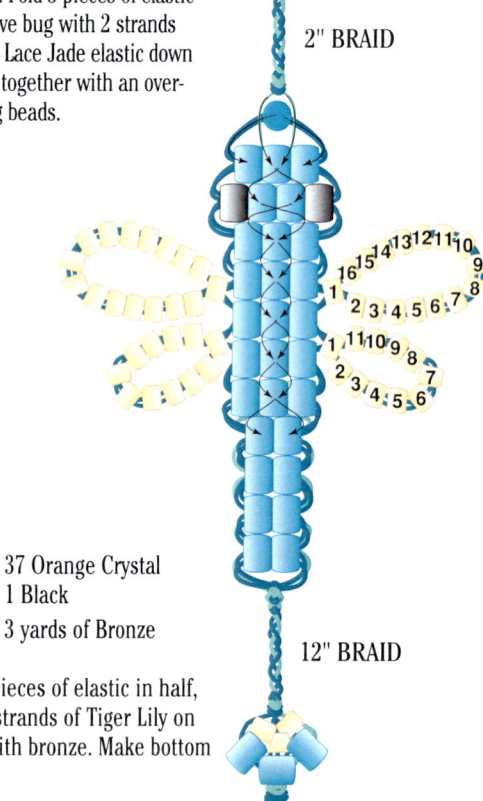

12" BRAID

Giraffe

BABY PONY BEADS:
105 Orange
34 Yellow
4 Black
1MM Rainbow Elastic:
9 yards of Sunshine

GIRAFFE: Cut elastic in 3 equal pieces, fold in half. Weave giraffe with 3 strands on each side to bottom of head. Leaving 2 strands loose, finish weaving with 2 strands on each side. Pick up 2 loose strands and lace down center beads of neck adding a bead between each row. Tie off.

9½" B

Fish

BABY PONY BEADS:
50 Yellow Crystal
18 Red Crystal
37 Orange Crystal
1 Black
1MM Rainbow Elastic:
6 yards of Tiger Lily
3 yards of Bronze

FISH: Cut tiger Lily in half. Fold 3 pieces of elastic in half, make top braid. Weave fish with 2 strands of Tiger Lily on each side. Lace down back beads with bronze. Make bottom braid adding beads.

2½" BRAID

12" BRAID

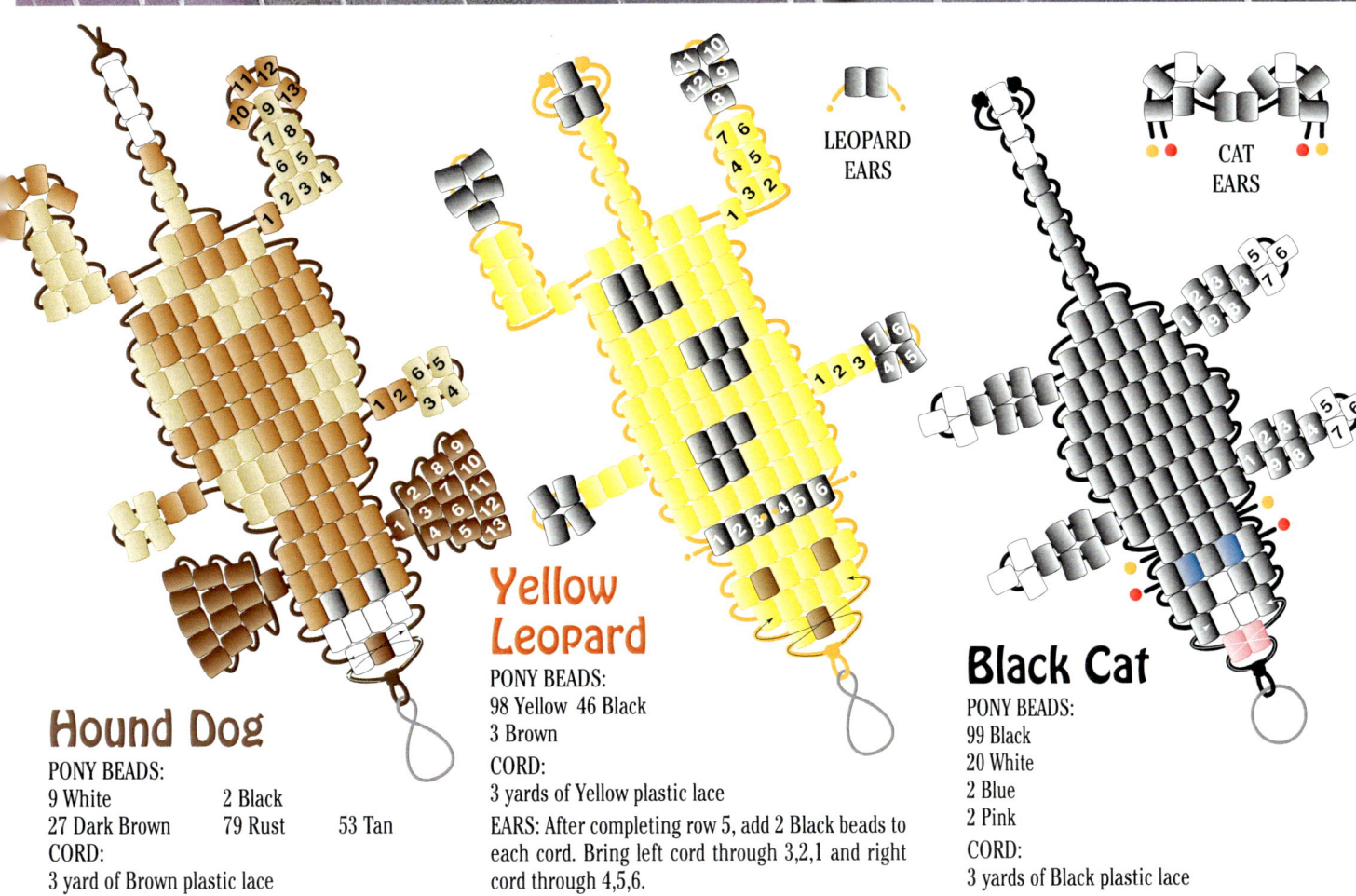

Hound Dog

PONY BEADS:

9 White	2 Black
27 Dark Brown	79 Rust
53 Tan	

CORD:

3 yard of Brown plastic lace

Yellow Leopard

PONY BEADS:

98 Yellow 46 Black

3 Brown

CORD:

3 yards of Yellow plastic lace

EARS: After completing row 5, add 2 Black beads to each cord. Bring left cord through 3,2,1 and right cord through 4,5,6.

LEOPARD EARS

Black Cat

PONY BEADS:

99 Black

20 White

2 Blue

2 Pink

CORD:

3 yards of Black plastic lace

CAT EARS

Magic Bus...
Moves Curious Kids
to Magical Museums

by Delores Frantz

Pony Beads: 52 Yellow, 8 Red, 8 Black
Lace: 2 yards of Black plastic noodle
Begin: Overhand knot and lanyard hook
Finish: Overhand knots

Flower
Power...

by Dawn Maier

Pony Beads: 30 Yellow,
  5 Red, 17 Lime Green
Lace: 2 yards of Yellow
  plastic lanyard
Begin: Overhand knot
  and lanyard hook
Finish: Overhand knot

Sunflower..

photo on page 17
Pony Beads: 61 Yellow,
  15 Brown, 28 Green
Lace: 2 yards of Yellow
  plastic lanyard
Begin: Lark's head knot
  and split ring
Finish: Overhand knot

Make beaded friends with eye and hair colors to match your favorite people!

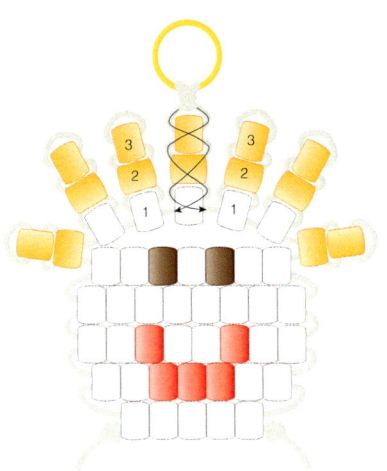

Tommy Towhead...
Likes to Leap
into Bed

Pony Beads:
14 Orange, 33 White Pearl, 2 Brown, 5 Red
Lace: 2 yards of White plastic lanyard
Begin: Lark's head knot and split ring
Finish: Overhand knots

Spiky Mikey...
Rides a Tricky
Trikey

Pony Beads: 14 Black, 2 White Pearl,
5 Orange, 33 Brown
Lace: 2 yards of Black plastic noodle
Begin: Lark's head knot and split ring
Finish: Overhand knots

Marvelous Marvin...
Loves Whistle Carvin'

Pony Beads: 14 Brown, 2 White Pearl,
5 Neon Orange, 33 Tortoise
Lace: 2 yards of Black plastic noodle
Begin: Lark's head knot and split ring
Finish: Overhand knots

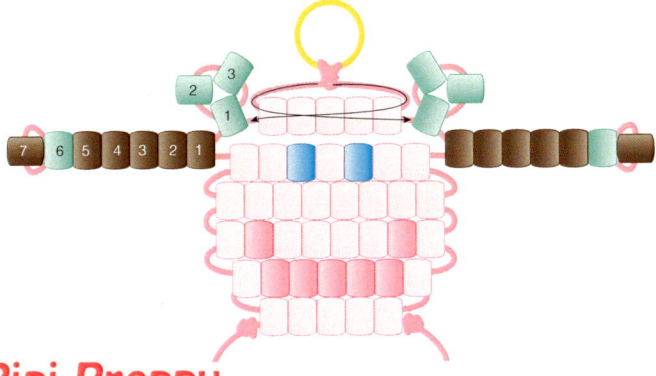

Pipi Preppy...
Is Perfectly Peppy

by Pam Pence

Pony Beads: 8 Green, 31 Pink Pearl, 2 Light Blue, 7 Neon Pink, 12 Brown
Lace: 2 yards of Pink plastic lanyard
Begin: Lark's head knot and split ring
Finish: Overhand knots

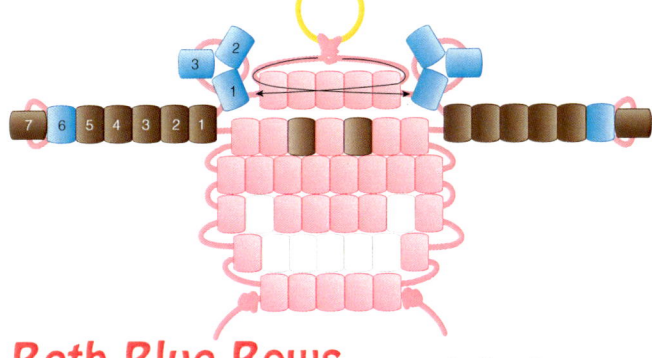

Beth Blue Bows...
Can Touch Her Toes

by Pam Pence
photo on page 17

Pony Beads: 8 Blue Pearl, 31 Pink, 14 Brown, 7 White Pearl
Lace: 2 yards of Pink plastic noodle
Begin: Lark's head knot and split ring
Finish: Overhand knots

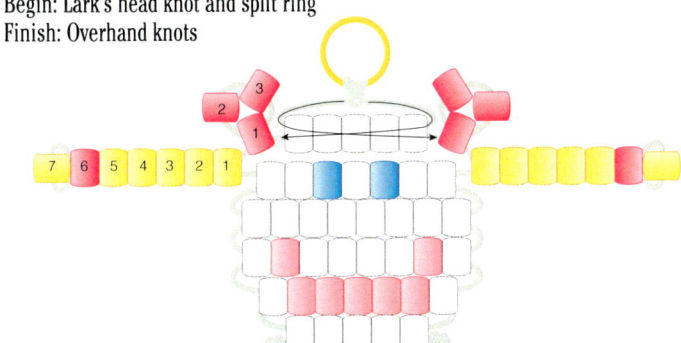

Polly Pigtails...
Polishes Colorful Toe Nails

by Pam Pence

Pony Beads: 8 Red, 31 White Pearl, 2 Blue Pearl, 7 Neon Pink, 12 Yellow
Lace: 2 yards of White plastic noodle
Begin: Lark's head knot and split ring
Finish: Overhand knots

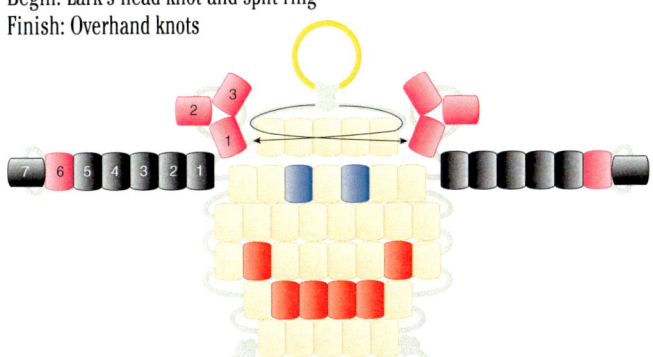

Smiling Sally...
Is Sometimes So Silly

by Pam Pence
photo on page 17

Pony Beads: 6 Red, 31 Ivory, 2 Blue, 8 Neon Pink, 12 Black
Lace: 2 yards of White plastic lanyard
Begin: Lark's head knot and split ring
Finish: Overhand knots

Watermelon...Makes Mouths Water

by Delores Frantz

Pony Beads: 48 Red, 19 White, 5 Black, 26 Green
Lace: 2 yards of Green plastic lanyard
Begin: Lark's head knot and split ring
Finish: Overhand knots

Up, Up and Away... Fly Kites on a Windy Day

by Virginia Reynolds

Pony Beads: 14 Green,
  13 Yellow, 48 Red
Lace: 2 yards of Red plastic lanyard
Begin: Lark's head knot and split ring
Finish: Make the kite tail

Pandy...Loves Candy

by Dawn Maier

Pony Beads: 58 white, 56 Black, 1 Pink
Lace: 2 yards of White plastic lanyard
Begin: Lark's head knot and split ring
Finish: Overhand knots

Pretty in Pink...

by Dawn Maier

Pony Beads: 5 Neon Yellow,
30 Neon Pink, 28 Neon Green
Lace: 2 yards of Pink plastic noodle
Begin: Make circle first, add petals.
Finish: Overhand knots

Flower Child... Blooms Where He is Planted

by Vicki Montgomery

Pony Beads: 35 Neon Yellow, 21 Neon Pink, 40 Neon Green
Lace: 2 yards of Yellow plastic lanyard
Begin: Make circle first, add petals.
Finish: Overhand knot

Petal Face...

by Vicki Montgomery

Pony Beads: 60 white, 12 Neon Orange, 12 Yellow, 22 Green
Lace: 2 yards of White plastic noodle
Begin: Make circle first, add petals.
Finish: Overhand knot

Beadie Babies
Cute and Clever Critters to Collect!

by Denise Sims

Fast-Track Froggie

PONY BEADS:
49 Green
2 Black
6 Yellow
CORD:
2 yards of Green yarn

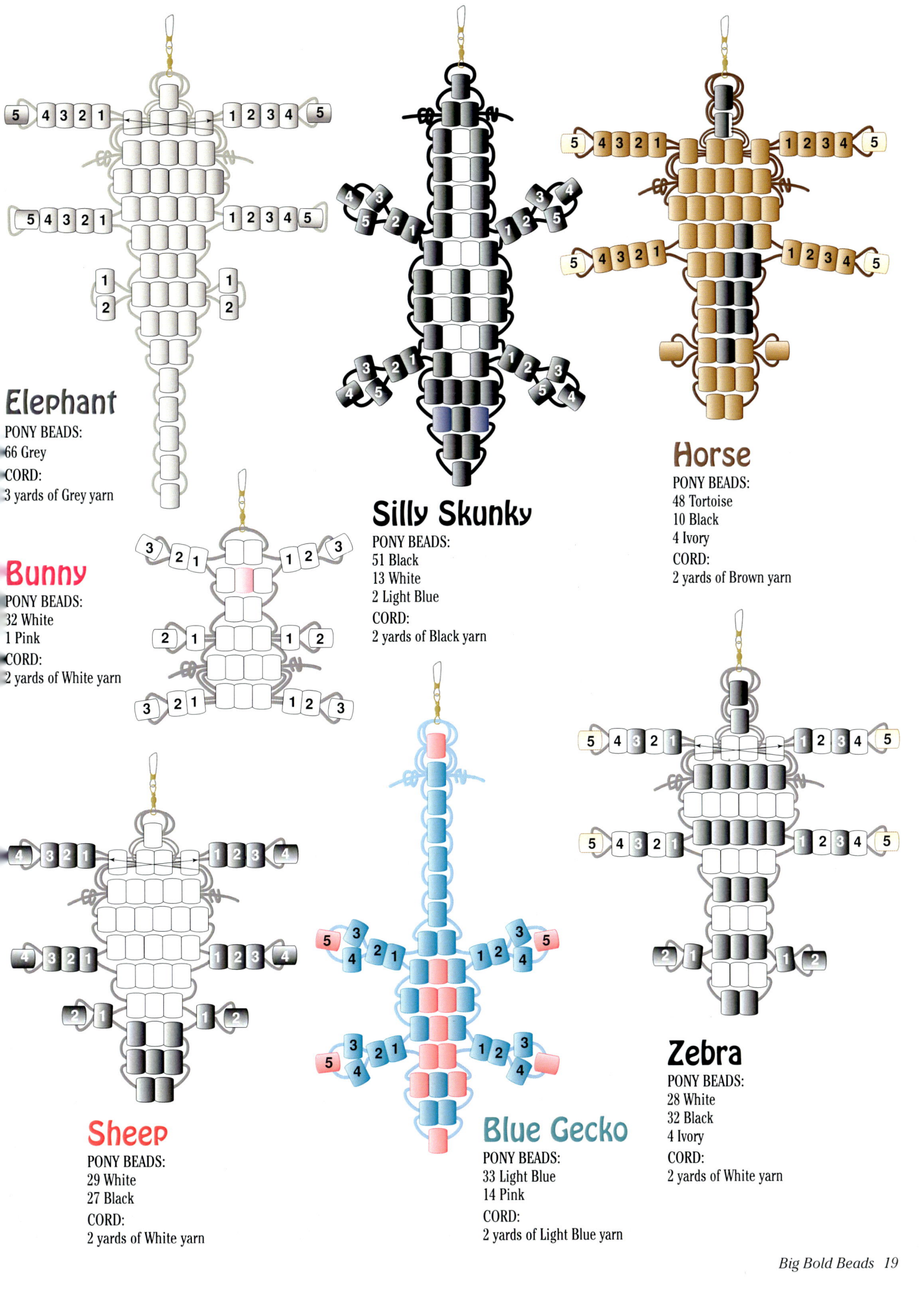

Elephant

PONY BEADS:
66 Grey

CORD:
3 yards of Grey yarn

Bunny

PONY BEADS:
32 White
1 Pink

CORD:
2 yards of White yarn

Silly Skunky

PONY BEADS:
51 Black
13 White
2 Light Blue

CORD:
2 yards of Black yarn

Horse

PONY BEADS:
48 Tortoise
10 Black
4 Ivory

CORD:
2 yards of Brown yarn

Sheep

PONY BEADS:
29 White
27 Black

CORD:
2 yards of White yarn

Blue Gecko

PONY BEADS:
33 Light Blue
14 Pink

CORD:
2 yards of Light Blue yarn

Zebra

PONY BEADS:
28 White
32 Black
4 Ivory

CORD:
2 yards of White yarn

Wonderful Projects for All Ages!

Additional Books to Inspire Creativity...

3401

3463

3442

3441

No. 3451

ISBN: 978-1-57421-328-7

EAN

9 781574 213287